The
Rabbi's Heartbeat

BRENNAN MANNING

NAVPRESS

Bringing Truth to Life

NavPress
P.O. Box 35001
Colorado Springs, CO 80935

The Navigators is an international Christian organization. Our mission is to reach, disciple, and equip people to know Christ and to make Him known through successive generations. We envision multitudes of diverse people in the United States and every other nation who have a passionate love for Christ, live a lifestyle of sharing Christ's love, and multiply spiritual laborers among those without Christ.

NavPress is the publishing ministry of The Navigators. NavPress publications help believers learn biblical truth and apply what they learn to their lives and ministries. Our mission is to stimulate spiritual formation among our readers.

ISBN 1-57683-469-7
Limited Edition, with CD 1-57683-598-7

Cover and interior design by David Carlson Design
Cover photograph: Deborah Raven/Photonica
Creative Team: Dan Rich, Scharlotte Rich, Greg Clouse

Some of the anecdotal illustrations in this book are true to life and are included with the permission of the persons involved. All other illustrations are composites of real situations, and any resemblance to people living or dead is coincidental.

This book incorporates content originally published in *Abba's Child* copyright © 1994, 2002 by Brennan Manning and published by NavPress.

Published in association with the literary agency of Alive Communications, Inc., 7680 Goddard Street, Suite 200, Colorado Springs, Colorado, 80920.

Unless otherwise identified, all Scripture quotations in this publication are taken from *The New Jerusalem Bible* (NJB), © 1985 by Darton, Longman & Todd, Ltd., and Doubleday & Company, Inc. Other versions used include: the HOLY BIBLE: NEW INTERNATIONAL VERSION® (NIV®), Copyright © 1973, 1978, 1984 by International Bible Society, used by permission of Zondervan Publishing House, all rights reserved.

Manning, Brennan.
  The rabbi's heartbeat / Brennan Manning.
     p. cm.
Includes bibliographical references.
  ISBN 1-57683-469-7
  1. Christian life. 2. Jesus Christ--Person and offices. I. Title.
  BV4501.3.M255 2003
  248.4--dc21
                          2003008314

Printed in Canada

1 2 3 4 5 6 7 8 9 10 / 07 06 05 04 03

FOR A FREE CATALOG OF
NAVPRESS BOOKS & BIBLE STUDIES,
CALL 1-800-366-7788 (USA)
OR 1-416-499-4615 (CANADA)

CONTENTS

he Rabbi doesn't want us to be perfect, just real. Yet at times we try so hard to please God and impress others— determined to be perfect Christians—that we're sucked dry of energy and sickened by our own slick surface and inner hypocrisy. It leaves us feeling dangerously brittle, as lifeless and fruitless as a tree in midwinter swoon.

We need a divine transfusion. The Rabbi's heartbeat is *for* us, not *against* us. Though He will always cut away the counterfeit green and barrenness of our hypocrisy, He will never crush the bruised reed of our broken lives. The hewn branches He leaves along the pathway are never the result of disgust but always the result of His care-filled pruning.

Come then, with Brennan, and listen to the Rabbi's heartbeat; lean in close to the warm reality of what His incarnation and resurrection can mean in the routines of your life. Feel the vitality that returns to your soul when you accept yourself, receive His love, and revel in His grace.

"I dry up the green tree and make the dry tree flourish" (Ezekiel 17:24).

Introduction

"How great is the love the Father has lavished on us,

that we should be called children of God!

And that is what we are."

1 John 3:1

"No thought can contain Him, no word can express Him;
He is beyond anything we can intellectualize or imagine."

B. MANNING

"I have come that they might have life, and that they
might have it more abundantly."

JOHN 10:10

❧

he dark riddle of life is illuminated in Jesus; the meaning, purpose, and goal of everything that happens to us, and the way to make it all count can only be learned from the Way, the Truth, and the Life. Nothing that exists can exist beyond the pale of His presence, nothing is irrelevant to it, nothing is without significance in it.

The sorrow of God lies in our fear of Him, our fear of life, and our fear of ourselves. As a father gathers his children into his arms at the end of a long and tiring day, so God longs to draw us into His embrace. No matter what your past or present, come; lean back in the shelter of His love and listen to the Rabbi's heartbeat. Let Him teach you about life, death, and eternity as Abba's beloved child. Take an unflinching look at yourself as you really are. Then look at who you are meant to become as you travel this earth as a child of God on the journey called life.

PART 1

Living True

✿

"Don't try to hold God's hand; let Him hold yours.
Let Him do the holding and you do the trusting."

H. WILLIAM WEBB-PEPLOE

"And now here is my secret, a very simple secret:
It is only with the heart that one can see rightly;
what is essential is invisible to the eye."

ANTOINE DE SAINT-EXUPERY

CHAPTER ONE

SAFE

"Quit keeping score altogether and surrender yourself with all your sinfulness to God who sees neither the score nor the scorekeeper but only his child redeemed by Christ."

THOMAS MERTON

"Living out of the false self creates a compulsive desire to present a perfect image to the public so that everybody will admire us and nobody will know us."

B. MANNING

dam and Eve hid, and we all have used them as role models. God calls us to stop hiding and come openly to Him. Why do we hide?

Simon Tugwell, in his book *The Beatitudes*, explains:

> We either flee our own reality or manufacture a
> false self which is mostly admirable, mildly prepos-
> sessing, and superficially happy. We hide what we
> know or feel ourselves to be (which we assume to be
> unacceptable and unlovable) behind some kind of
> appearance which we hope will be more pleasing.
> We hide behind pretty faces, which we put on for
> the benefit of our public. And in time we may
> even forget that we are hiding, and think that our
> assumed pretty face is what we really look like.[1]

God is the father who ran to his prodigal son when he came limping home. God weeps over us when shame and self-hatred immobilize us. God loves who we really are — whether we like it or not, and calls us, as He did Adam, to come out of hiding into a safe place. No amount of spiritual makeup can render us more presentable to Him. "Come to Me now," Jesus says. "Acknowledge and accept who I want to be for you: a Savior of boundless compassion, infinite patience, unbearable forgiveness, and love that keeps no score of wrongs."

It used to be that I never felt safe with myself unless I was performing flawlessly. Unwittingly I had projected onto God my feelings about myself. I felt safe with Him only when I saw myself as noble, generous, and loving, without scars, fears, or tears. Perfect!

Then, one radiant morning on a retreat deep in the Colorado Rockies, I came out of hiding. Jesus removed the shroud of perfectionist performance and, forgiven and free, I ran home. For I knew that Someone was waiting for me. Gripped in the depth of my soul, tears streaming down my cheeks, I internalized and finally felt all the words I had written and spoken about stubborn, unrelenting Love. That morning I understood that the words are but straw compared to the Reality. I leaped from simply being the teacher of God's love to becoming Abba's delight. I said goodbye to feeling frightened and said shalom to feeling safe.

What does it mean to feel you are in a safe place? That afternoon I wrote in my journal:

To feel safe is to stop living in my head and sink down into my heart and feel liked and accepted…not having to hide anymore and distract myself with books, television, movies, ice cream, shallow conversation…staying in the present moment and not escaping into the past or projecting into the future, alert and attentive to the now…feeling relaxed and not nervous or jittery…no need to impress or dazzle others or draw attention to myself…Unselfconscious, a new way of being with myself, a new way of being in the world…calm, unafraid, no anxiety about what's going to happen next…loved and valued…just being together as an end in itself.

Father God,

Thank you for calling to me when I am hiding from You and everyone else, including myself. Thank you that when I was matted and muddy with sin You loved me and looked for me to return home. Thank you for giving me a safe place within the unconditional love of Christ. Amen.

"I shall be very happy to make my weakness my special boast
that the power of Christ may stay over me."

2 CORINTHIANS 12:9

❧

CHAPTER TWO

BELOVED

"The disciple Jesus loved was reclining next to Jesus....
He leaned back on Jesus' breast."

JOHN 13:23, 25

"I knew there was only one place to go.
I sank down into the center of my soul, grew still,
and listened to the Rabbi's heartbeat."

B. MANNING

rom the first moment of our existence our most power-ful yearning is to fulfill the original purpose of our lives like the song — "to see Him more clearly, love Him more dearly, follow Him more nearly." We are made for God and nothing else will really satisfy us. The deepest desire of our hearts is for union with God.

Seek out a true contemplative — not a person who hears angelic voices and has fiery visions of the cherubim, but the person who encounters God with naked trust. What will that man or woman tell you? Thomas Merton, in *The Hidden Ground of Love*, responds, "Surrender your poverty and acknowledge your nothingness to the Lord. Whether you understand it or not, God loves you, is present in you, lives in you, dwells in you, calls you, saves you and offers you an understanding and compassion which are like nothing you have ever found in a book or heard in a sermon." [2]

Loving Father,
Help me experience the reality that I am the one
Jesus loves. Amen.

CHAPTER THREE

FORGIVEN

"What happens when we sin and fail...when life falls through the cracks?"

B. MANNING

"Faith is the courage to accept acceptance."

B. MANNING

One of the most shocking contradictions in the American church is the intense dislike many disciples of Jesus have for themselves. They are more displeased with their own shortcomings than they would ever dream of being about someone else's.

When I was eight, the impostor, or false self, was born as a defense against pain. The impostor within whispered, "Brennan, don't ever be your real self anymore because nobody likes you as you are. Invent a new self that everybody will admire and nobody will know." So I became a good boy — polite, well mannered, unobtrusive, and deferential. I studied hard, scored excellent grades, won a scholarship in high school, and was stalked every moment by the terror of abandonment and the sense that nobody was there for me.

The great divorce between my head and my heart endured throughout my ministry. For eighteen years I proclaimed the good news of God's passionate, unconditional love — utterly convicted in my head but not feeling it in my heart. I never felt loved. But finally, after an intensive soul-searching retreat, I came to understand that I was truly loved. As I finally grasped this immense truth, I began sobbing. As I drained the cup of grief, a remarkable thing happened: In the distance I heard music and dancing. I was the prodigal son limping home, not a spectator but a participant. The impostor faded, and I was in touch with my true self as the returned child of God.

"Come to Me now," Jesus says. "Quit projecting onto Me your own feelings about yourself. At this moment your life is a bruised reed and I will not crush it, a smoldering wick and I will not quench it. You are in a safe place." You are loved.

> Abba,
> Thank you for loving me in my sin and brokenness.
> Thank you for calling me Your child just as I am.
> Draw me ever closer to Your loving arms even when
> I push away and protest that I am not worthy. Thank
> you for running to greet me even as I finally turn
> toward home. Amen.

"A bruised reed he will not break and a smoldering wick he will not snuff out until he leads justice to victory."

MATTHEW 12:20; ISAIAH 42:3

❖

WOUNDED HEALERS

"What is denied cannot be healed."

B. MANNING

"In Love's service, only wounded soldiers can serve."

THORNTON WILDER

In the play "The Angel That Troubled the Waters," based on John 5, Thornton Wilder dramatizes the power of the pool of Bethesda to heal people whenever an angel stirred its waters. An ailing physician pleads for help but an angel insists that this healing is not for him. The angel says, "Without your wounds where would your power be? ...In Love's service, only wounded soldiers can serve."

Christians who remain in hiding continue to live the lie. We deny the reality of our sin. In a futile attempt to erase our past, we deprive the community of our healing gift. If we conceal our wounds, out of fear or shame, our inner darkness can neither be illuminated nor become a light for others. But when we dare to live as forgiven men and women, we join the wounded healers and draw closer to Jesus.

As we come to grips with our own selfishness and stupidity, we make friends with the impostor and accept that we are impoverished and broken and realize that, if we were not, we would be God. The art of gentleness toward ourselves leads us to be gentle with others — and is a natural prerequisite for our presence to God in prayer.

In *The Wounded Healer*, Henri Nouwen implies that grace and healing are communicated through the vulnerability of men and women who have been fractured and heartbroken by life. Alcoholics Anonymous is a community of wounded healers. Psychiatrist James Knight wrote:

> These persons have had their lives laid bare and
> pushed to the brink of destruction by alcoholism
> and its accompanying problems. When these persons
> arise from the ashes of the hellfire of addictive
> bondage, they have an understanding, sensitivity,
> and willingness to enter into and maintain healing
> encounters with their fellow alcoholics. In this
> encounter they cannot and will not permit them-
> selves to forget their brokenness and vulnerability.
> Their wounds are acknowledged, accepted, and kept
> visible. Further, their wounds are used to *illuminate*
> and stabilize their own lives while they work to bring
> the healing of sobriety to their alcoholic brothers
> and sisters, and sometimes to their sons and daugh-
> ters. The effectiveness of AA's members in the care
> and treatment of their fellow alcoholics is one of the

great success stories of our time, and graphically illustrates the power of wounds, when used creatively, to lighten the burden of pain and suffering.[3] *(emphasis added)*

Rainer Maria Rilke, in *Letters to a Young Poet*, explains the efficacy of his own gift: "Do not believe that he who seeks to comfort you lives untroubled among the simple and quiet words that sometimes do you good. His life has much difficulty and sadness and remains far behind yours. Were it not otherwise he would never have been able to find these words."[4]

Rilke's own wounds of pain and sadness made him aware of his inner poverty and created an emptiness that became the free space into which Christ could pour His healing power. Here was an echo of the cry of Paul: "I shall be very happy to make my weaknesses my special boast that the power of Christ may stay over me" (2 Corinthians 12:9).

The decision to come out of hiding is our initiation rite into the healing ministry of Jesus Christ. It brings its own reward. We stand in the Truth that sets us free and live out of the Reality that makes us whole.

Abba,

You are the Great Physician. Please heal my wounds. Let me join the wounded healers and reach out to others in need. Amen.

⁂

"God has a history of using the insignificant to accomplish the impossible."

RICHARD EXLEY

"Measure your life by loss instead of gain
Not by the wine drunk, but by the wine poured forth
For love's strength standeth in love's sacrifice
And whosoever suffereth most hath most to give."

HUDSON TAYLOR

CHAPTER FIVE

THE IMPOSTOR

"What a wretched man I am!"

ROMANS 7:24

"Every one of us is shadowed by an illusory person: a false self."

THOMAS MERTON

"This is love, not that we loved God but that he loved us and sent his Son as an atoning sacrifice for our sins."

1 JOHN 4:10

❧

homas Merton's notion of sin focuses not primarily on individual sinful acts but on a fundamental option for a life of pretense. Living out of the false self creates a compulsive desire to present a perfect image to the public so that everybody will admire us and nobody will know us. "There can only be two basic loves," wrote Augustine, "the love of God unto the forgetfulness of self, or the love of self unto the forgetfulness of God."

Merton said that a life devoted to the shadow is a life of sin. I have sinned in my cowardly refusal — out of fear of rejection — to think, feel, act, respond, and live from my authentic self. We even refuse to be our true self with God — and then wonder why we lack intimacy with Him.

Hatred of the impostor is actually self-hatred. The impostor and I constitute one person. Contempt for the false self gives vent to hostility, which manifests itself as general irritability — an irritation at the same faults in others that we hate in ourselves. Self-hatred always results in some form of self-destructive behavior.

Accepting the reality of our sinfulness means accepting our authentic self. Judas could not face his shadow; Peter could. The latter befriended the impostor within; the former raged against him. When we accept the truth of what we really are and surrender it to Jesus Christ, we are enveloped in peace, whether or not we feel ourselves to be at peace. By that I mean the peace that passes understanding is not a subjective sensation of peace; if we are in Christ, we are in peace even when we feel no peace.

The Master says to us: "Burn the old tapes spinning 'round in your head that bind you up and lock you into a self-centered stereotype. Listen to the new song of salvation written for those who know they are poor. Let go of your fear of the Father and your dislike of yourself. The father of lies twists the truth and distorts reality. He is the author of cynicism and skepticism, mistrust and despair, sick thinking and self-hatred. I am the Son of Compassion. You belong to Me and no one will tear you from My hand."

Jesus discloses God's true feelings toward us. As we turn the pages of the Gospels, we discover that the people Jesus encounters there are you and me. The understanding and compassion He offers them, He also offers you and me.

At the end of that special retreat in Colorado I wrote a letter to myself, to my impostor. I closed it by writing, "The longer you spend in the presence of Jesus, the more accustomed you grow to His face, the less adulation you will need because you will have discovered for yourself that He is Enough. And in the Presence, you will delight in the discovery of what it means to live by grace and not by performance."

Abba Father,
It gives us joy to know that as Your children we can speak honestly with You any time, any place, under any circumstance. We do not have to wear masks but can come to You openly, dirty and ragged, with all our sins and brokenness. Thank you for Your all-covering grace through Jesus Christ. Amen.

❧

"If anyone acknowledges that Jesus is the Son of God,
God lives in him and he in God. And so we know
and rely on the love God has for us."

1 JOHN 4:15-16

CHAPTER SIX

ORDINARY PEOPLE

"For God loved the world so much that he gave his only Son that who ever believes in him will have eternal life."

JOHN 3:16

"Define yourself radically as one beloved by God."

JOHN EAGAN

ohn Eagan, who died in 1987, was an ordinary man. An unheralded high school teacher, he spent thirty years ministering with youth. He never wrote a book, appeared on television, converted the masses, or gathered a reputation for holiness. He ate, slept, drank, biked cross-country, roamed through the woods, taught classes, and prayed. And he kept a journal, published shortly after his death. It is the story of an ordinary man whose soul was seduced and ravished by Jesus Christ.

The book's introduction reads, "The point of John's journal is that we ourselves are the greatest obstacles to our own nobility of soul — which is what sanctity means. We judge ourselves unworthy servants. And that judgment becomes a self-fulfilling prophecy. We deem ourselves too inconsiderable to be used even by a God capable of doing miracles with no more than mud and spit. And thus our false humility shackles an otherwise omnipotent God."[5]

Eagan, a flawed man with salient weaknesses and character defects, learned that brokenness is proper to the human condition, that we must forgive ourselves for being unlovable, inconsistent, incompetent, irritable, and potbellied. He knew that his sins could not keep him from God. They had all been redeemed by the blood of Christ. In his repentance he took his shadow self to the cross and dared to live as a forgiven man.

Struggling to shrink the illusory self, Eagan pursued a life of contemplative prayer with ruthless fidelity. During his annual, silent eight-day directed retreat he was visiting with his spiritual director:

> [The director] states something that I will ponder for years; he says it very deliberately. I ask him to repeat it so that I can write it down. "John, the heart of it is this: to make the Lord and his immense love for you constitutive of your personal worth. *Define yourself radically as one beloved by God.* God's love for you and his choice of you constitute your worth. Accept that, and let it become the most important thing in your life."
>
> We discuss it. The basis of my personal worth is not my possessions, my talents, not esteem of others, reputation...not kudos of appreciation from parents and kids, not applause, and everyone telling you how important you are to the place...I stand anchored

now in God before whom I stand naked, this God
who tells me, "You are my son, my beloved one."[6]
(*emphasis added*)

The ordinary self is the extraordinary self—the inconspicuous
nobody who shivers in the cold of the winter and sweats in the
heat of summer, who wakes up unreconciled to the new day, who
sits before a stack of pancakes, weaves through traffic, bangs
around in the basement, shops in the supermarket, pulls weeds
and rakes up the leaves, makes love and snowballs, flies kites and
listens to the sound of rain on the roof.

While the impostor draws his identity from past achievements
and the adulation of others, the true self claims identity in its
belovedness. We encounter God in the ordinariness of life: not
in the search for spiritual highs and extraordinary mystical
experiences but in our simple presence in life.

God created us for union with Himself. This is the original
purpose of our lives. And God is defined as love (1 John 4:16).
Living in an awareness of our belovedness is the axis around which
the Christian life revolves. Being the beloved is our identity, the
core of our existence. It is not merely a lofty thought. It is the

name by which God knows us, and the way He relates to us (Revelation 2:17).

If I must seek an identity outside of myself, then the accumulation of wealth, power, and honors allures me. Or I may find my center of gravity in interpersonal relationships. When I draw life and meaning from any other source than my belovedness, I am spiritually dead. When God gets relegated to second place behind any bauble or trinket, I have swapped the pearl of great price for painted fragments of glass.

"Who am I?" asked Thomas Merton, and he responded, "I am one loved by Christ."[7]

Mike Yaconelli, cofounder of Youth Specialties, tells about the time when, dejected and demoralized, he made a five-day retreat to a religious community for the mentally and physically handicapped, under the preaching of Henri Nouwen.

Yaconelli tells his story:

> Finally I accepted my brokenness....I knew I was broken. I knew I was a sinner. I knew I continually disappointed God, but I could never accept that part of me. It was a part of me that embarrassed me. I

continually felt the need to apologize, to run from my weaknesses, to deny who I was and concentrate on who I should be. I was broken, yes, but I was continually trying to never be broken again — or at least get to the place where I was very seldom broken....

At L'Arche, it became very clear to me that I had totally misunderstood the Christian faith. I came to see that it was in my brokenness, in my powerlessness, in my weakness that Jesus was made strong. It was in the acceptance of my lack of faith that God could give me faith. It was in the embracing of my brokenness that I could identify with others' brokenness. It was my role to identify with others' pain, not relieve it. Ministry was sharing, not dominating; understanding, not theologizing; caring, not fixing....

There is an anticipation, an electricity about God's presence in my life that I have never experienced before. I can only tell you that for the first time in my life I can hear Jesus whisper to me every day, "Michael, I love you. You are beloved." And for some strange reason, that seems to be enough.[8]

We are looking not at some spiritual giant of the Christian tradition, but at an ordinary evangelical man who has encountered the God of ordinary people. The God who grabs scalawags and ragamuffins by the scruff of the neck and raises them up to seat them with the princes and princesses of His people. Is this miracle enough for anybody? Or has the thunder of "God loved the world so much" been so muffled by the roar of religious rhetoric that we are deaf to the word that God could have tender feelings for us?

Define yourself radically as one beloved by God. This is the true self. Every other identity is illusion.

❧

"Repent and believe in the gospel, Jesus says. Turn around and believe that the good news that we are loved is better than we ever dared hope, and that to believe in that good news, to live out of it and toward it, to be in love with that good news, is of all glad things in this world the gladdest thing of all. Amen, and come, Lord Jesus."

FREDERICK BUECHNER

CHAPTER SEVEN

SOLITUDE

"Silent solitude forges true speech."

B. MANNING

"Failure to recognize the value of mere being with God,
as the beloved, without doing anything, is to gouge
the heart out of Christianity."

EDWARD SCHILLEBEECKX

Silence is not simply the absence of noise or the shutdown of communication with the outside world, but rather the process of coming to stillness. Silent solitude forges true speech. I'm not speaking of physical isolation; solitude here means being alone with the Alone, experiencing the transcendent Other and growing in awareness of one's identity as the beloved. It is impossible to know another person intimately without spending time together. Silence makes this solitude a reality. It has been said, "Silence is solitude practiced in action."

It is much like the story of a harried executive who went to a desert father and complained about frustration in prayer, flawed virtue, and failed relationships. The hermit went into his cave and came out with a basin and a pitcher of water. As he poured the water into the container the water splashed and was turbulent. Finally it began to settle and became smooth and placid. "That is the way it is when you live constantly in the midst of others," said the hermit. "You do not see yourself as you really are because of all the confusion and disturbance. You fail to recognize the divine presence in your life and the consciousness of your belovedness slowly fades."

It takes time for the water to settle. Coming to interior stillness requires waiting. Any attempt to hasten the process only stirs up the water anew.

Guilt feelings may arise immediately. The shadow self insinuates that you are selfish, wasting time, and evading the responsibilities of family, career, ministry, and community.

But silent solitude makes true speech possible and personal. If I am not in touch with my own belovedness, then I cannot touch the sacredness of others. If I am estranged from myself, I am likewise a stranger to others.

Experience has taught me that I connect best with others when I connect with the core of myself. When I allow God to liberate me from unhealthy dependence on people, I listen more attentively, love more unselfishly, and am more compassionate and playful. I take myself less seriously, become aware that the breath of the Father is on my face and that my countenance is bright with laughter in the midst of an adventure that I thoroughly enjoy.

Conscientiously "wasting" time with God enables me to speak and act from greater strength, to forgive rather than nurse the latest bruise to my wounded ego, to be capable of magnanimity during the petty moments of life. It empowers me to lose myself, at least temporarily, against a greater background than the tableau of my fears and insecurities, to merely be still and know that God is God.

As a fringe benefit, practicing silent solitude enables us to sleep less and feel more energetic. The energy expended in the impostor's exhausting pursuit of illusory happiness is now available to be focused on the things that really matter — love, friendship, and intimacy with God. The "still, small voice" is what you need to hear.

♣

"I asked for words! Life led me to a wood,
set me in solitude where speech is still and wisdom comes by prayer."

CHESTER B. EMERSON

"When Jesus heard what had happened,
he withdrew by boat to a solitary place."

MATTHEW 14:13

PART 2

Living Rooted in Love

❦

"God's Spirit touches our spirits and confirms who we really are. We know who he is, and we know who we are: Father and children."

ROMANS 8:16

CHAPTER EIGHT

ADOPTED

"Think of the love the Father has lavished on us,
by letting us be called God's children; and that is what we are."

1 JOHN 3:1

In His human journey, Jesus experienced God in a way that no prophet of Israel had ever dreamed or dared. Jesus was indwelt by the Spirit of the Father and given a name for God that would scandalize both the theology and public opinion of Israel, the name that escaped the mouth of the Nazarene carpenter: *Abba.*

Jewish children used this intimate colloquial form of speech in addressing their fathers. As a term for divinity, however, it was unprecedented not only in Judaism but in any of the great world religions. Joachim Jeremias wrote, "Abba, as a way of addressing God, is *ipsissima vox*, an authentic original utterance of Jesus. We are confronted with something new and astounding. Herein lies the great novelty of the gospel."[1] Jesus, the Beloved Son, does not hoard this experience for Himself. He invites and calls us to share the same intimate and liberating relationship.

Paul wrote, "For all who are led by the Spirit of God are children of God. For you did not receive a spirit of slavery to fall back into fear but you have received a spirit of adoption. When we cry, 'Abba,' it is that spirit bearing witness with our spirit that we are children of God" (Romans 8:14-16). John, "the disciple Jesus loved," exclaims, "Think of the love the Father has lavished on us, by letting us be called God's children; and that is what we are" (1 John 3:1).

The greatest gift I have ever received from Jesus Christ has been the Abba experience. My dignity as Abba's child is my most coherent sense of self.

Years ago, I related a story about a priest from Detroit named Edward Farrell who visited his uncle in Ireland on his eightieth birthday. On the great day, they got up before dawn and went walking in silence along the shores of Lake Killarney and stopped to watch the sunrise. After they stood, side by side staring at the rising sun, suddenly the uncle turned and went skipping down the road. He was radiant, beaming, smiling from ear to ear.

His nephew said, "Uncle Seamus, you really look happy."

"I am, lad."

"Want to tell me why?"

His eighty-year-old uncle replied, "Yes, you see, my Abba is very fond of me."

How would you respond if I asked you this question? Do you honestly believe God likes you, not just loves you because theologically God has to love you?

Jesus, for "in his body lives the fullness of divinity"

(Colossians 2:9), singularly understands the tenderness and compassion of the Father's heart. Why did Jesus love sinners, ragamuffins and the rabble who knew nothing of the law? Because His Abba loved them. He did nothing on His own, but only what His Abba told Him. Through meal-sharing, preaching, teaching, and healing, Jesus acted out His understanding of the Father's indiscriminate love — a love that causes His sun to rise on bad men as well as good, and His rain to fall on honest and dishonest men alike (Matthew 5:45).

Because the shining sun and the falling rain are given both to those who love God and to those who reject God, the compassion of the Son embraces those who are still living in sin. The Pharisee lurking within all of us shuns sinners. Jesus turns toward them with gracious kindness. He sustains His attention throughout their lives for the sake of their conversion "which is always possible to the very last moment."[2]

Abba Father,
Thank you for loving me as Your child, no matter
what my condition. Amen.

"To all who did accept him he gave power to become children of God."

JOHN 1:12

❧

CHAPTER NINE

RADICAL LIFESTYLE

"A new command I give you. Love one another.
As I have loved you, so you must love one another. All men will know
that you are my disciples if you love one another."

JOHN 13:34-35

"Love your enemies and do good...and you will be sons of the Most High
for he himself is kind to the ungrateful and the wicked."

LUKE 6:35

"The way you are with others every day,
regardless of their status, is the true test of faith."

B. Manning

❖

God calls His children to a countercultural lifestyle of forgiveness in a world that demands an eye for an eye — and worse. But if loving God is the first commandment, and loving our neighbor proves our love for God, and if it is easy to love those who love us, then loving our enemies must be the filial badge that identifies Abba's children.

The summons to live as forgiven and forgiving children is radically inclusive. The demands for forgiveness are so daunting that they seem humanly impossible. The exigencies of forgiveness are simply beyond the capacity of ungraced human will. Only reckless confidence in a Source greater than ourselves can empower us to forgive the wounds inflicted by others. In boundary moments such as these there is only one place to go — Calvary.

Stay there for a long time and watch as Abba's Only Begotten dies utterly alone in bloody disgrace. Watch as He breathes forgiveness on His torturers at the moment of their greatest cruelty and mercilessness. On that lonely hill outside the city wall of old Jerusalem, you will experience the healing power of the dying Lord.

Experientially, the inner healing of the heart is seldom a sudden catharsis or an instant liberation from bitterness, anger, resentment, and hatred. More often it is a gentle growing into oneness with the Crucified who has achieved our peace through His blood on the cross. This may take considerable time because the memories are still so vivid and the hurt is still so deep. But it *will* happen. The crucified Christ is not merely a heroic example to the church: He is the power and wisdom of God, a living force in His present risenness, transforming our lives and enabling us to extend the hand of reconciliation to our enemies.

Understanding triggers the compassion that makes forgiveness possible. Author Stephen Covey recalled an incident while taking the subway one Sunday. On a quiet ride through New York City a man and his children burst onto the train. The children ran wild, shouting, screaming, and wrestling, while their father made no attempt to intervene.

Finally Covey turned to the father and said, "Sir, perhaps you could restore order here by telling your children to come back and sit down."

"I know I should do something," the man replied. "We just came from the hospital. Their mother died an hour ago. I just don't know what to do."[3]

Our hearts of stone become hearts of flesh when we learn where others weep.

The sons and daughters of Abba are to be the most nonjudgmental people. They ought to get along famously with sinners.

Remember the passage in Matthew where Jesus says, "Be perfect as your heavenly father is perfect"? In Luke, the same verse is translated, "Be compassionate as your heavenly Father is compassionate." Biblical scholars say that the two words, *perfect* and *compassionate*, can be reduced to the same reality. Conclusion: To follow Jesus in His ministry of compassion precisely defines the biblical meaning of being perfect as the heavenly Father is perfect.

My identity as Abba's child is not an abstraction or a tap dance into religiosity. It is the core truth of my existence. Living in the wisdom of accepted tenderness profoundly affects my perception of reality, the way I respond to people and their life situations.

How I treat my brothers and sisters from day to day, whether they be Caucasian, African, Asian, or Hispanic; how I react to the sin-scarred wino on the street; how I respond to interruptions from people I dislike; how I deal with ordinary people in their ordinary unbelief on an ordinary day will speak the truth of who I am more poignantly than the pro-life sticker on the bumper of my car.

The compassionate life is neither a sloppy goodwill toward the world not the plague of what Robert Wicks calls "chronic niceness." The way of tenderness avoids blind fanaticism. Instead, it seeks to see with penetrating clarity. The compassion of God in our hearts opens our eyes to the unique worth of each person. "The other is 'ourself'; and we must love him in his sin as we were loved in our sin."[4]

This is the unceasing struggle of a lifetime. It is the long and painful process of becoming like Christ in the way I choose to think, speak, and live each day. "God's love is not a conditional love; it is an open-hearted, generous self-giving which God offers to men. Those who would carefully limit the operation of God's love…have missed the point."[5]

Abba,

Help me to see people with Your eyes. Remind me
that I am forgiven much. Fill me to overflowing
with Your Holy Spirit so that I can pour out love
to others. Amen.

"But I tell you who hear me: Love your enemies,

do good to those who hate you,

bless those who curse you,

pray for those who mistreat you....

Do not judge, and you will not be judged.

Do not condemn, and you will not be condemned.

Forgive, and you will be forgiven.

Give and it will be given to you.

A good measure, pressed down, shaken together

and running over, will be poured into your lap.

For with the measure you use,

it will be measured to you."

Luke 6:27, 37-38 NIV

❧

CHAPTER TEN

PERFECT LOVE

"Do not be afraid, for I have redeemed you;
I have called you by name, you are mine."

ISAIAH 43:1

"It is God who has called us by name.
The God beside whose beauty the Grand Canyon is only
a shadow has called us beloved."

B. MANNING

"As the Father has loved me, so I have loved you.

Remain in my love."

JOHN 15:9

❧

uppose for a moment that in a flash of insight you discovered that all your motives for ministry were essentially egocentric, or suppose that last night you got drunk and committed adultery, or suppose that you failed to respond to a cry for help and the person committed suicide. What would you do?

Would guilt, self-condemnation, and self-hatred consume you or would you jump into the water and swim at breakneck speed toward Jesus? Haunted by feelings of unworthiness, would you allow the darkness to overcome you or would you let Jesus be who He is — a Savior of boundless compassion and infinite patience, a Lover who keeps no score of our wrongs?

Many of us can recall an utterly unpredictable moment in which we were deeply affected by an encounter with Jesus Christ — a peak experience that brought immense consolation and heartfelt joy. We were swept up in wonder and love. Quite simply, we were infatuated with Jesus, in love with love. For me the experience lasted nine years.

Then, shortly after ordination, I got shanghaied by success. Applause and acclaim in the ministry muffled the voice of the Beloved. I was in demand. What a giddy feeling to have my person admired and my presence required! As my unconditional availability increased and intimacy with Christ decreased, I rationalized that this was the price to be paid for unstinting service to the Kingdom enterprise.

Years later, the fame faded and my popularity waned. When rejection and failure first made their unwelcome appearance, I was spiritually unequipped for the inner devastation. Loneliness and sadness invaded my soul. In search of a mood-altering experience, I unplugged the jug. With my predisposition to alcoholism, I was a raging drunk within eighteen months. I abandoned the treasure and took flight from the simple sacredness of my life.

Finally I went for treatment in Hazelden, Minnesota. As the alcoholic fog lifted, I knew there was only one place to go. I sank down into the center of my soul, grew still, and listened to the Rabbi's heartbeat.

What is the purpose of this disclosure? For anyone caught up in the oppression of thinking that God works only through saints, it offers a word of encouragement. For those who have fulfilled Jesus' prophetic word to Peter, "Before the cock crows you will have disowned me three times," it offers a word of liberation. For those trapped in cynicism, indifference, or despair, it offers a word of hope.

Jesus is the same yesterday, today, and forever (Hebrews 13:8). The way He related to Peter is the way He relates to us. The recovery of passion starts with reappraising the value of the treasure, continues with letting the Great Rabbi hold us against His heart, and comes to fruition in a personal transformation of which we will not even be aware.

❖

"In love there can be no fear,
but fear is driven out by perfect love: because to fear
is to expect punishment, and anyone who
is afraid is still imperfect in love."

1 JOHN 4:18

Abba,

Whenever I question who I am, help me to see my identity as "the one Jesus loves." As I go through my day, please keep reminding me. Help me treasure time to meet with You alone to know You well.

Amen.

CHAPTER ELEVEN

ON BEING
CHILDLIKE

"And he said: 'I tell you the truth, unless you change and
become like little children, you will never enter the kingdom of heaven.
Therefore, whoever humbles himself like this child is
the greatest in the kingdom of heaven. And whoever welcomes
a little child like this in my name welcomes me.'"

MATTHEW 18:3–5 NIV

*"Our inner child is not an end in itself
but a doorway into the depths of our union with our
indwelling God, a sinking down into the
fullness of the Abba experience, into the vivid
awareness that my inner child is Abba's child, held fast by Him,
both in light and in shadow."*

B. MANNING

n sharp contrast to the pharisaic perception of God and religion, the biblical perception of the gospel of grace is that of a child who has never experienced anything but love and who tries to do her best because she is loved. When she makes mistakes, she knows they do not jeopardize the love of her parents. The possibility that her parents might stop loving her if she doesn't clean her room never enters her mind. They may disapprove of her behavior, but their love is not contingent on her performance.

For the Pharisee the emphasis is always on personal effort and achievement. The gospel of grace emphasizes the primacy of God's love. The Pharisee savors impeccable conduct; the child delights in the relentless tenderness of God.

In response to her sister's question of what she meant "by remaining a little child before the good God," Therese of Lisieux said,

> It is recognizing one's nothingness, expecting everything from the good God, just as a little child expects everything from its father; it is not getting anxious about anything, not trying to make one's fortune....

Being little is also not attributing to oneself the
virtues that one practices, as if one believed oneself
capable of achieving something, but recognizing that
the good God puts this treasure into the hands of his
little child for it to make use of it whenever it needs
to; but it is always the good God's treasure. Finally, it
is never being disheartened by one's faults, because
children often fall, but they are too little to do
themselves much harm.[6]

Parents love a little one before that child makes his or her
mark in the world. The secure child's accomplishments later in life
are not the effort to gain acceptance and approval but the abun-
dant overflow of a sense of being loved.

The child spontaneously expresses emotions; the Pharisee
carefully represses them. To open yourself to another person…is
a sign of the dynamic presence of the Holy Spirit. To ignore,
repress, or dismiss our feelings is to fail to listen to the stirrings
of the Spirit within our emotional life. Jesus listened, cried, got
frustrated, righteously angry, and felt sorrow for people in pain.

We have spread so many ashes over the historical Jesus that we scarcely feel the glow of His presence anymore. He is a man in a way that we have forgotten men can be: truthful, blunt, emotional, non-manipulative, sensitive, compassionate—His inner child so liberated that He did not feel it unmanly to cry. He met people head on and refused to cut any deal at the price of His integrity. The gospel portrait of the beloved Child of Abba is that of a man exquisitely attuned to His emotions and uninhibited in expressing them. The Son of Man used feelings as sensitive emotional antennae to which He listened carefully and through which He perceived the will of His Father.

The face that a child wears is her own face, and her eyes that look on the world do not squint to try to see labels on people. The Pharisee within spends most of his time reacting to labels, his own and others'.

The positive qualities of the child—openness, trusting dependence, playfulness, simplicity, sensitivity to feelings—restrain us from closing ourselves off to new ideas, surprises of the Spirit, and risky opportunities for growth. My inner child is Abba's child, held fast by Him, both in light and in shadow.

Consider Frederick Buechner's words:

> We are children, perhaps, at the very moment when
> we know that it is as children that God loves us—not

because we have deserved his love and not in spite of our undeserving; not because we try and not because we recognize the futility of our trying; but simply because he has chosen to love us. We are children because he is our Father; and all our efforts, fruitful and fruitless, to do good, to speak truth, to understand, are the efforts of children who, for all their precocity, are children still in that before we loved him, he loved us, as children, through Jesus Christ our Lord.[7]

Abba,

Thank you for loving me as Your child through no merit of my own, just as I am. Thank you for watching over me in the dark and guarding and guiding my steps. Please help me to be more childlike in my life of faith. Amen.

PART 3

Living Under Grace

❦

"The mystery in a nutshell is just this:
Christ is in you, therefore you can look forward
to sharing in God's glory. It's that simple."

COLOSSIANS 1:27

CHAPTER TWELVE

RESURRECTION FAITH

"All I want to know is Christ and the power of his resurrection."

PHILIPPIANS 3:10

"Scripture presents only two alternatives:
either you believe in the resurrection and you believe
in Jesus of Nazareth or you don't believe in the resurrection
and you don't believe in Jesus of Nazareth."

B. MANNING

hat gives the teaching of Jesus its power? What distinguishes it from teachings from the Koran, Buddha, Confucius? The risen Christ does. For example, if Jesus did not rise we can safely praise the Sermon on the Mount as a magnificent ethic. If He did, such praise doesn't matter. The sermon becomes a portrait of our ultimate destiny. The transforming power of the Word resides in the risen Lord who stands by it. I will say it again: The dynamic power of the gospel flows from the resurrection. When through faith we fully accept that Jesus is who He claims to be, we experience the risen Christ. Scripture presents only two alternatives: Either you believe in the resurrection and you believe in Jesus of Nazareth, or you don't believe in the resurrection and you don't believe in Jesus of Nazareth.

For me, the most radical demand of Christian faith lies in summoning the courage to say "yes" to the present risenness of Jesus Christ. I have been a Christian for nearly fifty years. I have lived long enough to appreciate that Christianity is lived more in the valley than on the mountaintop, that faith is never doubt-free, and that although God has revealed Himself in creation and in history, the surest way to know God is, in the words of Thomas Aquinas, as *tamquam ignotum*, as utterly unknowable. No thought can contain Him, no word can express Him; He is beyond anything we can intellectualize or imagine.

My "yes" to the fullness of divinity embodied in the present risenness of Christ is scary because it is so personal. *Yes* is a bold word not to be taken lightly or spoken frivolously. This "yes" is an act of faith, a decisive, wholehearted response of my whole being to the risen Jesus present beside me, before me, around me, and within me; a cry of confidence that my faith in Jesus provides security not only in death but in the face of a worse threat posed by my own malice; a word that must be repeated over and over again in the ever-changing landscape of life.

Risen Lord Jesus,
Allow me to see the pieces of my life as all parts of
Your holy design. Help me to pay attention to Your
touch on my life and say "yes" to You as I go about
my days on this earth. Amen.

"The gospel proclaims a hidden power in the world —
the living presence of the risen Christ."

CHAPTER THIRTEEN

❖

RESURRECTION
FREEDOM

*"Now this Lord is the Spirit,
and where the Spirit of the Lord is, there is freedom."*

2 CORINTHIANS 3:17 NIV

*"Faith in the present risenness of Jesus carries with it
life-changing implications for the gritty routine of daily life."*

B. MANNING

he Spirit is the Easter gift of Jesus the Christ.[1] "In the evening of that same day, the first day of the week… Jesus came and stood among them. He said to them, 'Peace be with you….' After saying this he breathed on them and said, 'Receive the Holy Spirit' " (John 20:19, 22). In the oldest texts of 2 Corinthians 3:17 the risen Jesus is Himself called *pneuma*, Spirit: "Now this Lord is the Spirit, and where the Spirit of the Lord is, there is freedom."

The present risenness of Jesus as a "life-giving Spirit" means that I can cope with anything. I am not on my own. "I pray that you may realize…how vast are the resources of his Spirit available to us" (Ephesians 1:18-19). Relying not on my own limited reserves but on the limitless power of the risen Christ I can stare down not only the impostor and the Pharisee, but even the prospect of my impending death.

Our hope is inextricably connected with the conscious awareness of present risenness.

How does the life-giving Spirit of the Risen Lord manifest Himself on "hard days"? In our willingness to stand fast, our refusal to run away and escape into self-destructive behavior. Resurrection power enables us to engage in the savage confrontation with untamed emotions, to accept pain…however acute it may be. And in the process we discover that we are not alone, that we can stand fast in the awareness of present risenness and so become fuller, deeper, richer disciples.

"The mystery is Christ among you, your hope of glory" (Colossians 1:27). Hope knows that if great trials are avoided, great deeds remain undone and the possibility of growth into greatness of soul is aborted. Pessimism and defeat are never the fruit of the life-giving Spirit but rather reveal our unawareness of present risenness.

When tragedy makes its unwelcome appearance and we are deaf to everything but the shriek of our own agony, when courage flies out the window and the world seems to be a hostile, menacing place, it is the hour of our own Gethsemane. No word, however sincere, offers any comfort or consolation. The night is bad. Our minds are numb, our hearts vacant, our nerves shattered. How will we make it through the night? The God of our lonely journey is silent.

And yet it may happen in these the most desperate trials of our human existence that beyond any rational explanation, we may feel a nail-scarred hand clutching ours. We are able, as Etty Hillesun, the Dutch Jewess who died in Auschwitz in 1943, wrote, "to safe-guard that little piece of God in ourselves"[2] and not give way to despair. We make it through the night and darkness gives way to the light of morning. The tragedy radically alters the direction of our lives, but in our vulnerability and defenselessness we experience the power of Jesus in His present risenness.

Apart from the risen Christ we live in a world without mean-ing, a world of shifting phenomena, a world of death, danger, and darkness. A world of inexplicable futility. Nothing is intercon-nected. Nothing is worth doing for nothing endures. It is all sound and fury with no ultimate significance.[3]

The dark riddle of life is illuminated in Jesus; the meaning, purpose, and goal of everything that happens to us, and the way to make it all count can be learned only from the Way, the Truth, and the Life.

Living in the awareness of the risen Christ is not a trivial pur-suit for the bored and lonely or a defense mechanism enabling us to cope with the stress and sorrow of life. It is the key that unlocks the door to grasping the meaning of existence. All day and every day we are being reshaped into the image of Christ. Everything that happens to us is designed to this end. Nothing that exists can exist beyond the pale of His presence ("All things were created through him and for him"—Colossians 1:16), nothing is irrelevant to it, nothing is without significance in it.

Everything that is comes alive in the risen Christ. Everything— great, small, important, unimportant, distant, and near — has its place, its meaning, and its value. Through union with Him nothing is wasted. There is never a moment that does not carry eternal significance — no action that is sterile, no love that lacks fruition, and no prayer that is unheard.

> Abba,
> Thank you for holding out Your nail-scarred hand
> and walking with me in all the dark places. Thank
> you for causing me to grow into a fuller, deeper,
> richer walk with You as a disciple of Christ Jesus.
> Amen.

"We know that by turning everything to their good

God cooperates with all those who love him."

<small>ROMANS 8:28</small>

CHAPTER FOURTEEN

SHARING LIVING WATER

"I give you a new commandment:
Love one another as I have loved you."

JOHN 13:34

"In every encounter we either give life or we drain it.
There is no neutral exchange."

B. MANNING

resent risenness is the impulse to ministry. "When he saw the crowds he felt sorry for them because they were harassed and dejected, like sheep without a shepherd" (Matthew 9:36). This passage of exquisite tenderness offers a glimpse into the human soul of Jesus. It tells how He feels about human beings. It reveals His way of looking out on the world, His non-judgmental attitude toward people who were looking for love in wrong places and seeking happiness in wrong pursuits. It is a simple revelation that the heart of Jesus beats the same yesterday, today, and forever.

Every time the Gospels mention that Jesus was moved with deep emotion for people, they show that it led Him to do some-thing — physical or inner healing, deliverance or exorcism, feeding the hungry crowds or intercessory prayer. Above all it moved Him to dispel distorted images of who He is and who God is, to lead people out of darkness into light. Jesus' compassion moved Him to tell the story of God's love.

Our impulse to tell the salvation story arises from listening to the heartbeat of the risen Jesus within us. Telling the story does not require that we become ordained ministers or flamboyant street-corner preachers, nor does it demand that we try to convert people by concussion with one sledgehammer blow of the Bible after another. It simply means we share with others what our lives used to be like, what happened when we met Jesus, and what our lives are like now.

The impostor recoils at the prospect of telling the story because he fears rejection. He is tense and anxious because he must rely on himself; his power is limited by his paltry resources. He dreads failure.

The true self is not cowed by timidity. Buoyed up and carried on by a power greater than one's own, the true self finds basic security in the awareness of the present risenness of Jesus Christ. Jesus, rather than self, is always the indispensable core of ministry. "Cut off from me you can do nothing" (John 15:5). The moment we acknowledge that we are powerless, we enter into the liberating sphere of the Risen One and we are freed from anxiety over the outcome.

Perhaps when the final curtain falls, you will have told the story to only one person. God promises that one cup of living water drawn from the fountain and passed on to another will not go unrewarded.

Lord,

Touch me, fill me with Your Holy Spirit, and show

me how to reach out to those that You put in my

path. Amen.

CHAPTER FIFTEEN

THORNS AND THISTLES

"The one who calls you is faithful and he will do it."

1 THESSALONIANS 5:24 NIV

"Hope knows that if great trials are avoided,
great deeds remain undone and the possibility of growth
into greatness of soul is aborted."

B. MANNING

Sustaining ourselves in the awareness of the present risenness of Jesus is a costly decision that requires more courage than intelligence. I notice a tendency in myself to sink into unawareness, to enjoy some things alone, to exclude Christ, to hug certain experiences and relationships to myself. Exacerbated by what someone has called "the agnosticism of inattention"—the lack of personal discipline over media bombardment, shallow reading, sterile conversation, perfunctory prayer, and subjugation of the senses — the awareness of the risen Christ grows dim. Just as the failure to be attentive undermines love, confidence, and communion in a human relationship, so inattention to my true self hidden with Christ in God obscures awareness of the divine relationship. As the old proverb goes, "Thorns and thistles choke the unused path." A once verdant heart becomes a devastated vineyard.

When I shut Jesus out of my consciousness by looking the other way, the icy finger of agnosticism touches my heart. My agnosticism does not consist in the denial of a personal God; it is unbelief growing like lichen from my inattention to the sacred presence. The way I spend my time and money and the way I interact with others routinely testifies to the degree of my awareness or unawareness.

In *The Road Less Traveled*, Scott Peck wrote, "Without discipline we can solve nothing. With only some discipline we can solve some problems. With total discipline we can solve all problems."

With the passing of years I am growing more convinced that the discipline of awareness of the present risenness of Jesus is intimately linked to the recovery of passion.

> Lord Jesus,
> Teach me to weigh and measure the things I allow in
> my life, keeping only those that have eternal value.
> Amen.

"The unaware life is not worth living."

Socrates

PART FOUR

Living by Heart

"Jesus said, 'So, you believe because you've seen with your own eyes. Even better blessings are in store for those who believe without seeing.' "

JOHN 20:29

CHAPTER SIXTEEN

RECOVERING
PASSION

*"There have been times when I preferred cheap slivers
of glass to the pearl of great price."*

B. MANNING

*"The kingdom of heaven is like a treasure hidden in a field which some-
one has found; he hides it again, and goes off happy, sells everything he
owns and buys the field."*

MATTHEW 13:44

❧

he treasure is Jesus Christ. It is one thing to discover the
treasure and quite another to claim it as one's own through ruthless determination and tenacious effort.

The paltriness of our lives is largely due to our fascination
with the trinkets and trophies of the unreal world that is passing
away. Sex, drugs, booze, the pursuit of money, pleasure and
power, even a little religion, suppress the awareness of present
risenness. Whatever the addiction — be it a smothering relationship, a dysfunctional dependence, or mere laziness — our capacity
to be affected by Christ is numbed.

A story is told of a young Jewish boy named Mordecai who
had been dedicated to the Lord by his parents. Mordecai grew in

age and wisdom and grace but was rambunctious, loved the world, gulping down the days and dreaming through the nights. His parents sat him down and told him how important the Word of God was. But when it came time for him to go to the synagogue and learn the Word of God, he would not leave the lakes he loved to swim in and the trees he loved to climb. Nothing could persuade him.

But one day the Great Rabbi visited the village and asked to be left alone with the boy. To leave their son alone with this lion of a man terrified the parents, but they left him. He then picked up the boy and held him silently against his heart. The next day the boy began going to the synagogue before going to the woods and lakes and trees. And the Word of God became one with the words of Mordecai and the trees and the lake.

Mordecai grew up to become a great man who helped many people. And when they came to him he said, "I first learned the Word of God when the Great Rabbi held me silently against his heart."[1] Heart spoke to heart.

On a recent five-day silent retreat, I spent the entire time in John's gospel. Whenever a sentence caused my heart to stir I wrote it out longhand in a journal. The first of many entries was also the last: "The disciple Jesus loved was reclining next to Jesus...He leaned back on Jesus' breast" (John 13:23, 25). We must not hurry past this scene in search of deeper revelation, or we will miss a magnificent insight. John lays his head on the heart of God, on the breast of the Man whom the council of Nicea defined as "being coequal and consubstantial to the Father...God from God, Light from Light, True God from True God."

This can be a personal encounter, radically affecting our understanding of who God is and what our relationship with Jesus is meant to be. God allows a young Jew, reclining in the rags of his twenty-odd years, to listen to his heartbeat!

Have we ever seen the human Jesus at closer range?

Clearly, John was not intimidated by Jesus. He was not afraid of his Lord and Master. John was deeply affected by this sacred Man.

Fearing that I would miss the divinity of Jesus, I distanced myself from His humanity, like an ancient worshiper shielding his eyes from the Holy of Holies. But as John leans back on the breast of Jesus and listens to the heartbeat of the Great Rabbi, he comes to know Him in a way that surpasses mere cognitive knowledge. What a world of difference lies between *knowing about* someone and *knowing Him!*

In a flash of intuitive understanding, John experiences Jesus as the human face of the God who is love. And in coming to know who the Great Rabbi is, John discovers who he is—*the disciple Jesus loved*. For John the heart of Christianity was not an inherited doctrine but a message born of his own experience. And the message he declared was, "God is love" (1 John 4:16).

The recovery of passion begins with the recovery of my true self as the beloved. If I find Christ I will find myself and if I find my true self I will find Him. This is the goal and purpose of our lives. John did not believe that Jesus was the most important thing; he believed that Jesus was the *only* thing.

If John were to be asked, "What is your primary identity, your most coherent sense of yourself?" he would not reply, "I am a disciple, an apostle, an evangelist," but "I am the one Jesus loves."

To read John 13:23-25 without faith is to read it without profit. To risk the passionate life, we must be "affected by" Jesus as John was; we must engage His experience with our lives rather than our memories. Until I lay my head on Jesus' breast, listen to His heartbeat, and personally appropriate the Christ-experience of John's eyewitness, I have only a *derivative* spirituality. The Christ of faith is no less accessible to us in His present risenness than was the

Christ of history in His human flesh to the beloved disciple. To see Jesus in the flesh was an extraordinary privilege but "more blessed are they who have not seen and yet believed" (John 20:29).

Looking at Jesus through the prism of John's values offers unique insight into the priorities of discipleship. One's personal relationship with Christ towers over every other consideration. What establishes preeminence in the Christian community is not office, title, or territory, not the charismatic gifts of tongues, healing, or inspired preaching, but only our response to Jesus' question, "Do you love Me?"

⚜

"May all your expectations be frustrated, may all your plans be thwarted, may all your desires be withered into nothingness, that you may experience the powerlessness and poverty of a child and sing and dance in the love of God who is Father, Son, and Spirit."

LARRY HEIN

CHAPTER SEVENTEEN

SEEKING APPROVAL

"Am I now trying to win the approval of men, or of God?
Or am I trying to please men? If I were still trying to please men,
I would not be a servant of Christ."

GALATIANS 1:10 NIV

*"Lacking a lively awareness of my core identity
as Abba's child, it is relatively easy to become enslaved
to the approval and disapproval of others."*

B. MANNING

♣

nthony DeMello in *The Way to Love* wrote bluntly:

Look at your life and see how you have filled its emptiness with people. As a result, they have a stranglehold on you. See how they control your behavior by their approval and disapproval. They hold the power to ease your loneliness with their company, to send your spirits soaring with their praise, to bring you down to the depths with their criticism and rejection. Take a look at yourself spending almost every waking moment of your day placating and pleasing people, whether they are living or dead.[2]

In John's Gospel, the Jews are said to be incapable of believing because they "look to one another for approval" (John 5:44). There appears to be a radical incompatibility between human respect and authentic faith in Christ. The strokes or the scorn of our peers become more important than the approval of Jesus.

The opinions of others exert a subtle but controlling pressure on the words I speak and the words I stuff; the tyranny of my peers controls the decisions I make and the ones I refuse to make. I am afraid of what others may say.

Peter G. van Breeman identified this fear:

> This fear of ridicule paralyzes more effectively
> than would a head-on attack or an outspoken harsh
> criticism. How much good is left undone because
> of our fear of the opinion of others! We are immo-
> bilized by the thought: What will others say? The
> irony of all this is that the opinions we fear most are
> not those of people we really respect, yet those same
> persons influence our lives more than we want to
> admit. This enervating fear of our peers can create
> an appalling mediocrity.[3]

When we freely assent to the mystery of our belovedness and accept our core identity as Abba's child, we slowly gain autonomy from controlling relationships. We become *inner-directed* rather than *outer-determined*. The fleeting flashes of pleasure or pain caused by the affirmation or deprivation of others will never entirely disappear, but their power to induce self-betrayal will be diminished.

To own my own unique self in a world filled with voices contrary to the gospel requires enormous fortitude. In this age of much empty religious talk and proliferating Bible studies, idle intellectual curiosity and pretensions of importance, intelligence without courage is bankrupt. The truth of faith has little value when it is not also the life of the heart. Thirteenth-century theologian Anthony of Padua opened every class he taught with the phrase, *"Of what value is learning that does not turn to love?"*

The pressures of religious conformity and political correctness in our culture bring us face to face with what Johannes Metz called "the poverty of uniqueness." The poverty of uniqueness is the call of Jesus to stand utterly alone when the only alternative is to cut a deal at the price of one's integrity. It is a lonely "yes" to the whispers of our true self, a clinging to our core identity when companionship and community support are withheld. It is a courageous determination to make unpopular decisions that are expressive of the truth of who we are — not of who we think we should be or who someone else wants us to be. It is trusting enough in Jesus to make mistakes and believing enough that His life will still pulse within us. It is the unarticulated, gut-wrenching yielding of our true self to the poverty of our own unique, mysterious personality.

In the name of prudence the terrified impostor would have us betray our identity and our mission, whatever it might be — standing with a friend in the harsh weather of life, solidarity with the oppressed at the cost of ridicule, refusal to be silent in the face of injustice, unswerving loyalty to a spouse, or any lonely call to duty on a wintry night. Other voices clamor, "Don't make waves, say what everyone else is saying and do what they're doing, tailor your conscience to fit this year's fashion. When in Rome do as the Romans do. You don't want to raise eyebrows and be dismissed as a kook. Settle in and settle down. You'd be overruled anyway."

Anyone who has ever stood up for the truth of human dignity, no matter how disfigured, only to find previously supportive friends holding back, even remonstrating with you for your boldness, feels the loneliness of the poverty of uniqueness. This happens every day to those who choose to suffer for the absolute voice of conscience, even in what seem to be small matters. They find themselves standing alone. I have yet to meet the man or woman who enjoys such responsibility.

The measure of our depth-awareness of Christ's present risenness is our capacity to stand up for the truth and sustain the disapproval of significant others. We can no longer drift with the crowd or echo the opinions of others. The inner voice, "Take courage. It is I. Do not be afraid," assures that our security rests in having no security. When we stand on our own two feet and claim responsibility for our unique self, we are growing in personal autonomy, fortitude, and freedom from the bondage of human approval.

Abba,
Help me to live for Your approval only, desiring that
my life would please You in matters large and small.
Amen.

"The unwounded life bears no resemblance to the Rabbi."

B. MANNING

❧

CHAPTER EIGHTEEN

BEING AND DOING

"Everyone who listens to these words of mine and does not act on them is like a stupid man who built his house on sand."

MATTHEW 7:26

"Genuine faith leads to knowing the love of God, to confessing Jesus as Lord, and to being transformed by what we know."

B. MANNING

n recent decades both psychology and religion have laid strong emphasis on *being* over *doing*. In religious circles we have reacted sharply against the heresy of works and the pharisaical focus on the endless doing of ritual acts, which is the undoing of authentic religion. We have been cautioned not to identify ourselves with our career or ministry because when change comes with old age, sickness, or retirement, we will feel worthless and useless and without a clue as to who we are.

There is undeniable wisdom here. The tendency to construct a self-image based on performing religious acts easily leads to the illusion of self-righteousness. When our sense of self is tied to any particular task—such as serving in a soup kitchen, promoting environmental consciousness, or giving spiritual instruction—we take a functional approach to life, work becomes the central value; we lose touch with the true self and the happy combination of mysterious dignity and pompous dust which we really are.

And yet…

While acknowledging the truth contained in the foregoing paragraphs, I want to affirm that what we do may be far more decisive and far more expressive of the ultimate truth of who we *are* in Christ than anything else.

Substituting theoretical concepts for acts of love keeps life at a safe distance. This is the dark side of putting being over doing. Is this not the accusation that Jesus leveled against the religious elite of His day?

The Christian commitment is not an abstraction. It is a concrete, visible, courageous, and formidable way of being in the world forged by daily choices consistent with inner truth. A commitment that is not visible in humble service, suffering discipleship, and creative love is an illusion. Jesus Christ is impatient with illusions, and the world has no interest in abstractions. "Everyone who listens to these words of mine and does not act on them is like a stupid man who built his house on sand" (Matthew 7:26). If we bypass these words of the Great Rabbi, the spiritual life will be nothing more than fantasy.

The one who talks, especially if he talks to God, can affect a great deal, but the one who acts really means business and has more claims on our attention. If you want to know what a person really believes, don't just listen to what he *says*, watch what he *does*.[4]

Jesus reinforced His words with deeds. He was not intimidated by authority figures. He seemed unfazed by the crowd's complaints that He was violating the law by going to a sinner's house. Jesus broke the law of traditions when the love of persons demanded it.

At another point in His earthly ministry Jesus said, "The Son of Man has not come to be served but to serve." On the eve of His death, Jesus took off His outer garment, tied a towel around His waist, poured water into a copper basin, and washed the feet of His disciples. *The Jerusalem Bible* notes that the dress and duty are those of a slave.

A profound mystery: God becomes a slave. This implies very specifically that God wants to be known through servanthood.

John the beloved disciple presents a mind-bending image of God, blowing away all previous conceptions of who the Messiah is and what discipleship is all about. What a scandalous and unprecedented reversal of the world's values! To prefer to be the servant rather than the lord of the household is the path of downward mobility in an upwardly mobile culture. To taunt the idols of prestige, honor, and recognition, to refuse to take oneself seriously...to dance to the tune of a different drummer, and to freely embrace the servant lifestyle — these are the attitudes that bear the stamp of authentic discipleship.

The stark realism of John's portrait of Christ leaves no room for romanticized idealism or sloppy sentimentality. Servanthood is not an emotion or mood or feeling; it is a decision to live like Jesus. It has nothing to do with what we feel; it has everything to do with what we do — humble service.

When being is divorced from doing, pious thoughts become an adequate substitute for washing dirty feet.

The call to the servant lifestyle is both a warning not to be seduced by the secular standard of human greatness and also a summons to courageous faith. As we participate in the foot-washing experience, Jesus addresses us directly, commanding our complete attention as He looks into our eyes and makes this colossal claim: "If you want to know what God is like, look at Me. If you want to learn that your God does not come to rule but serve, watch Me. If you want assurance that you did not invent the story of God's love, listen to My heartbeat."

Abba,
Transform my heart into that of a true servant and show me how You would have me serve. Please make it obvious, as I am often slow to understand. Amen.

"The truth of faith has little value when it
is not also the life of the heart."

B. MANNING

CHAPTER NINETEEN

❧

DEATH AND LIFE

"Keep your own death before your eyes each day."

SAINT BENEDICT

"For this reason I remind you to fan into flame the gift of God,
which is in you....For God did not give us a spirit of timidity,
but a spirit of power, of love and of self-discipline."

2 TIMOTHY 1:6-7 NIV

ne imponderable trait of the human psyche is its ability to make irrational judgments about worthwhile human investments along with its refusal to view life in light of eternity. Whether it be the grandiosity of the addict, the self-importance of the workaholic, the self-interest of the movie mogul, or the self-absorption of the average person in his or her plans and projects — all collaborate to weave the fantasy of invincibility, or what Ernest Becker calls "the denial of death."

For many the separation from loved ones is too painful to consider. Perhaps, for most of us, the frantic pace of life and the immediate claims of the present moment leave no time, except for fleeting reflection at funerals, to contemplate seriously where we came from and where we are going.

Saint Benedict, the founder of Western monasticism, offers the sober advice to "keep your own death before your eyes each day." It not a counsel to morbidity but a challenge to faith and fortitude. Until we come to terms with this primal fact of life, as Parker Palmer noted, there can be no spirituality worth speaking of.

I waffle back and forth between fear and anticipation of death. I am most afraid of death when I am most afraid of life. When I'm conscious of my belovedness and when I am alert to the present risenness of Jesus, I can face death courageously. Paul's boast that life, of course, means Christ and death is a prize to be won (Philippians 1:21) becomes my own. Without fear I can acknowledge that the authentic Christian tension is not between life and death but between life and life. I buoyantly affirm the Great Rabbi's words on the eve of His death: "I live, and you will live" (John 14:19). Above all, when He holds me silently against His heart, I can even accept the terror of abandonment.

But when the night is darkest and the impostor is running amok, and I am thinking how well I have done and how necessary I am and how secure I feel in the affirmation of others and how remarkable that I've become a player in the religion thing and how deserving I am of an exotic vacation and how proud my family is of me and how glorious the future looks — suddenly, like mist rising from the fields, I am enveloped in thoughts of death. Then I am afraid. I know that behind all my Christian slogans and conversations about the resurrection, there lurks a very frightened man.

When we hear the footsteps of the grim reaper, our perception of reality changes dramatically. With precious time slipping away like sand in an hourglass, we quickly dismiss all that is petty and irrelevant and focus only on matters of ultimate concern. As Samuel Johnson once said, "The prospect of being hanged concentrates a man's mind wonderfully." Although a panic attack might be our initial response, we soon realize that sobbing is a waste of time.

In her novel, *The Nice and the Good*, Iris Murdoch depicts a man trapped in a cave as the water is rising. He thinks, "If I ever get out of here I will be no man's judge...not to judge, not to be superior, not to exercise power, not to seek, seek, seek. To love and to reconcile and to forgive, only this matters. All power is sin and all law is frailty. Love is the only justice. Forgiveness, reconciliation, not law."[5]

The denial of death is not a healthy option for a disciple of Christ. Nor is pessimism in the face of today's troubles. The significant shift in priorities that comes through living twenty-four hours at a time is not mere resignation to what we know cannot be changed. My life in the confrontation with trials and tribulations is not stoic passivity. My death-defying "no" to despair at the end of my life and my life-affirming "yes" to seemingly insurmountable problems in the midst of my life are both animated by hope in the invincible might of the risen Jesus Christ and in "the immeasurable scope of His power in us who believe" (Ephesians 1:19).

We are not cowed into timidity by death and life. Were we forced to rely on our own shabby resources we would be pitiful people indeed. But the awareness of Christ's present risenness persuades us that we are buoyed up and carried on by a life greater than our own.

The Christ within who is our hope of glory is not a matter of theological debate or philosophical speculation. He is not a hobby, a part-time project, a good theme for a book, or a last resort when all human effort fails. He is our life, the most real fact about us. He is the power and wisdom of God dwelling within us.

The wise teacher William Johnston wrote to a young colleague, "Never banish the thought of death from your consciousness."[6] To those brave souls who long to forego fantasy for a life of fortitude I would add, "Never deliberately banish the awareness of present risenness...[but] a moment listen to the Rabbi's heartbeat."

Abba,
Keep the thought of death in my consciousness as a
reminder of the seriousness and joy of life. My hope
is in the invincible power and might of the risen
Christ who overpowered death that I might truly live.
Amen and come soon Lord Jesus.

CHAPTER TWENTY

RECONCILIATION

"I shall see you again, and your hearts will be full of joy."

JOHN 16:22

"The promised peace that the world cannot give is located
in being in right relationship with God."

B. MANNING

*"God's love is not conditional. We cannot do anything
to deserve God's love — for which reason it is called grace;
and we need not do anything to provoke it.
It is already there. Any love that is going to be salvific
must be of this type, absolutely unconditional and free."*

BEATRICE BRUTEAU

*"If we search for one word to describe
the mission and ministry of Jesus Christ,
reconciliation would not be a bad choice."*

B. MANNING

❧

he unaffected heart is one of the dark mysteries of human existence. It beats dispassionately in human beings with lazy minds, listless attitudes, unused talents, and buried hopes. They never seem to get beneath the surface of their lives. They die before they learn to live.

Years wasted in vain regrets, energies dissipated in haphazard relationships and projects, emotions blunted, passive before whatever experiences the day brings, they are like snoring sleepers who resent having their peace disturbed. Their existential mistrust of God, the world, and even themselves underlies their inability to make a passionate commitment to anyone or anything.

The unaffected heart leaves a legacy of Disney World paraphernalia and a thousand lost golf balls. The sheer vacuity of the unlived life guarantees the person will never be missed. "These people, living on borrowed emotions, stumbling through the corridors of time like shipboard drunks...never taste life deeply enough to be either saints or sinners."[7]

Paul Claudel once stated that the greatest sin is to lose the sense of sin. If sin is merely an aberration caused by oppressive social structures, circumstances, environment, temperament, compulsions, and upbringing, we will admit the sinful human condition but deny that we are sinners. We see ourselves as basically nice, benevolent people with minor hang-ups and neuroses that are the common lot of humanity. We rationalize and minimize our terrifying capacity to make peace with evil and thereby reject all that is not nice about us.

The essence of sin lies in the enormity of our self-centeredness, which denies our radical contingency and displaces the sovereignty of God with what Alan Jones calls "our sucking two-percent self." Our fascination with power, prestige, and possessions justifies aggressive self-assertion, regardless of the damage inflicted on others. The impostor insists that looking out for Numero Uno is the only sensible posture in a dog-eat-dog world. Unless and until we face our sanctimonious viciousness, we cannot grasp the meaning of the reconciliation Christ affected on Calvary's hill. We cannot receive what the crucified Rabbi has to give unless we admit our plight and stretch out our hands until our arms ache.

If we search for one word to describe the mission and ministry of Jesus Christ, *reconciliation* would not be a bad choice. "In other words, God in Christ was reconciling the world to himself, not holding men's faults against them" (2 Corinthians 5:19).

The lives of those fully engaged in the human struggle will be riddled with bullet holes. Whatever happened in the life of Jesus is in some way going to happen to us. Wounds are necessary. The soul has to be wounded as well as the body. To think that the natural and proper state is to be without wounds is an illusion.[8] Those who wear bulletproof vests to protect themselves from failure, shipwreck, and heartbreak will never know what love is. The unwounded life bears no resemblance to the Rabbi.

Shortly after I entered seminary, I went to a priest and told him about the innumerable bouts of heavy drinking during my three years in the Marine Corps and how I grieved over time squandered in self-indulgence. To my surprise he smiled and said, "Rejoice and be glad. You will have a heart of compassion for those who walk that lonely road. God will use your brokenness to bless many people." We need not be eaten alive by guilt. We can stop lying to ourselves. The reconciled heart says that everything that has happened to me had to happen to make me who I am — without exception.

Thomas Moore adds this insight: "Our depressions, jealousies, narcissism, and failures are not at odds with the spiritual life. Indeed they are essential to it. When tended, they prevent the spirit from zooming off into the ozone of perfectionism and spiritual pride."[9]

Only in a relationship of the deepest intimacy can we allow a person to know us as we truly are. It is difficult enough to live with the awareness of our stinginess and shallowness, our anxieties and infidelities, but to disclose our dark secrets to another is intolerably risky. The impostor does not want to come out of hiding. He will grab for the cosmetic kit and put on his pretty face to make himself "presentable." Whom can I level with? To whom can I bare my soul? I cannot admit that I have done wrong; I cannot admit that I have made a huge mistake, except to someone who I know accepts me.

Our salvation and strength lie in complete trust in the Great Rabbi who broke bread with the outcast Zacchaeus. His meal-sharing with a notorious sinner was not merely a gesture of liberal tolerance and humanitarian sentiment. It embodied His mission and His message: forgiveness, peace, and reconciliation for all, without exception.

The promised peace that the world cannot give is located in being in a right relationship with God. Self-acceptance becomes possible only through radical trust in Jesus' acceptance of me as I am. And the meaning of the Rabbi's words, "Behold, I make all things new," becomes luminously clear.

Those who have opened the door to Jesus, reclined at the table, and listened to His heartbeat will experience at least four things. First, listening to the Rabbi's heartbeat is immediately a Trinitarian experience. The moment you press your ear against His heart, you instantly hear Abba's footsteps in the distance. I do not know how this happens. It just does. It is a simple movement from intellectual cognition to experiential awareness that Jesus and the Father are one in the Holy Spirit, the bond of infinite tenderness between them.

Second, we realize that we are not alone on the Yellow Brick Road. Traffic is heavy. Fellow travelers are everywhere. It isn't just me and Jesus anymore. The road is dotted with the moral and the immoral, the beautiful and the grungy...and the Rabbi's word, of course, is to love each person along the way.

Third, when we recline at the table with Jesus we will learn that the recovery of passion is intimately connected with the discovery of the passion of Jesus.

An extraordinary transaction takes place between Jesus and Peter on the Tiberian seashore...in the form of a heart-stopping question: "Do you love Me?" What is going on here? The Jesus who died a bloody, God-forsaken death that we might live, is asking if we love Him!

The vulnerability of God in permitting Himself to be affected by our response and the heartbreak of Jesus as He wept over Jerusalem for not receiving Him are utterly astounding. When God comes streaming into our lives in the power of His Word, all He asks is that we be stunned and surprised, let our mouths hang open, and begin to breathe deeply.

Fourth, the awareness dawns that God is totally Other. We are in the magisterial presence of God. Faith stirs and our fear and trembling find their voice once more. In worship we move into the tremendous poverty that is the adoration of God. We have moved from the Upper Room where John had laid his head on the breast of Jesus to the book of Revelation where the beloved disciple fell prostrate before the Lamb of God.

Let the Great Rabbi hold you silently against His heart. In learning who He is, you will find out who you are: Abba's child in Christ our Lord.

"Today on planet earth, may you experience the wonder and beauty of yourself as Abba's Child and temple of the Holy Spirit through Jesus Christ our Lord. Amen."

LARRY HEIN

❧

Notes

PART 1

1. Simon Tugwell, *The Beatitudes: Soundings in Christian Tradition* (Springfield, IL: Templegate Publishers, 1980), p. 130.

2. Thomas Merton, *The Hidden Ground of Love: Letters* (New York: Farrar, Strauss, Giroux, 1985), p. 146.

3. James A. Knight, M.D., *Psychiatry and Religion: Overlapping Concerns*, Lillian Robinson, M.D., ed. (Washington, DC: American Psychiatric Press, 1986).

4. Rainer Maria Rilke, *Letters to a Young Poet* (New York: W. W. Norton, 1962), quoted by Knight, p. 36.

5. John Eagan, *A Traveler Toward the Dawn* (Chicago: Loyola University Press, 1990), p. xii.

6. Eagan, pp. 150-151.

7. James Finley, *Merton's Palace of Nowhere* (Notre Dame, IN: Ave Maria Press, 1978), p. 96.

8. Mike Yaconelli, "The Back Door" column, *The Door*.

PART 2

1. Joachim Jeremias, *The Parables of Jesus* (New York: Charles Scribner, 1970), p. 128.

2. Hans Kung, *On Being a Christian* (New York: Doubleday, 1976), p. 33.

3. Stephen Covey, *The Seven Habits of Highly Effective People*, Audio Cassette Seminar (Provo, UT).

4. Robert J. Wicks, *Touching the Holy* (Notre Dame, IN: Ave Maria Press, 1992), p. 87.

5. J. B. Phillips, *New Testament Christianity* (London: Hodder & Stoughton, Ltd. and New York: The Macmillan Co., n.d.), n.p.

6. Therese of Lisieux, quoted by Simon Tugwell, *The Beatitudes: Soundings in Christian Traditions* (Springfield, IL: Templegate Publishers, 1980), p. 138.

7. Frederick Buechner, *The Magnificent Defeat* (San Francisco: Harper and Row, 1966), p. 135.

PART 3

1. Edward Schillebeeckx, *For the Sake of the Gospel* (New York: Crossroad, 1992), p. 73.

2. William Barry, *God's Passionate Desire and Our Response* (Notre Dame, IN: Ave Maria Press, 1993), p. 87.

3. Don Aelred Watkin, *The Heart of the World* (London: Burns and Dates, 1954), p. 94.

PART 4

1. John Shea, *Starlight* (New York: Crossroad, 1993), pp. 115-117.

2. Anthony DeMello, *The Way to Love* (New York: Doubleday, 1991), p. 64.

3. Peter G. van Breeman, *Called By Name* (Denville, NJ: Dimension Books, 1976), p. 88.

4. James Mackey, *Jesus: The Man and the Myth* (New York: Paulist Press, 1979), p. 148.

5. Iris Murdoch, *The Nice and the Good* (New York: Penguin Books, 1978), p. 315.

6. William Johnston, *Being in Love* (San Francisco: Harper and Row, 1989), p. 99.

7. Eugene Kennedy, *The Choice to Be Human* (New York: Doubleday, 1985), p. 14.

8. Thomas Moore, *The Care of the Soul* (San Francisco: Harper Collins, 1992), p. 263.

9. Moore, p. 112.

AUTHOR

BRENNAN MANNING is a writer and speaker who leads spiritual retreats for people of all ages and backgrounds. He is the author of numerous books, including the best-seller *Abba's Child*. A resident of New Orleans, he travels extensively in the U.S. and abroad to share the good news of the unconditional love of God.